SE - - '15

Pebble® Plus

> DESTRUCTION <

BLOW IT UP!

by Thomas Kingsley Troupe

Consulting Editor: Gail Saunders-Smith, PhD

CAPSTONE PRESS
a capstone imprint

Pebble Plus is published by Capstone Press,
1710 Roe Crest Drive, North Mankato, Minnesota 56003
www.capstonepub.com

Library of Congress Cataloging-in-Publication Data
Troupe, Thomas Kingsley.
 Blow it up! / by Thomas Kingsley Troupe.
     p. cm. —(Pebble plus. Destruction)
 Audience: 006-008.
 Audience: K to grade 3.
 Summary: "Large, colorful photos and simple text illustrate structures being imploded"—Provided by publisher.
 Includes bibliographical references and index.
 ISBN 978-1-4765-2086-5 (library binding)—ISBN 978-1-4765-3487-9 (ebook pdf)
1. Wrecking—Juvenile literature. 2. Blasting—Juvenile literature. I. Title.
 TH447.T76 2014
 690'.26—dc23
                                                                                                2013002439

Editorial Credits
Erika L. Shores, editor; Heidi Thompson, designer; Marcie Spence, media researcher; Kathy McColley, production specialist

Photo Credits
AP Images: Danny Johnston, 7, Stew Milne, 17, 19, The Indianapolis Star, from the WTHR Chopper, Alan Petersime, 13, 15, The Winchester Star, Scott Mason, cover; Shutterstock: Howard Sandler, 21, Luke Schmidt, back cover, 1, 5, 9, 11, VectorZilla, design element

Note to Parents and Teachers

The Destruction set supports social studies standards related to science, technology, and society. This book describes and illustrates the demolition of structures. The repetition of words and phrases helps early readers learn new words. This book also introduces early readers to subject-specific vocabulary words, which are defined in the Glossary section. Early readers may need assistance to read some words and to use the Table of Contents, Glossary, Read More, Internet Sites, and Index sections of the book.

Printed in China by Nordica.
0314/CA21400181
022014   007226NORDF13

Table of Contents

Blow It Up!

The empty building downtown
is old and unsafe.

Time to blow it up!

Demolition &
Implosion

5

Workers place explosives

inside the building.

An explosion blows

the building to pieces.

KaBOOM!

The building falls down.

Look at the huge dust cloud!

A Stadium Falls

The old stadium is falling apart.

Explosives will clear the area

for a new field.

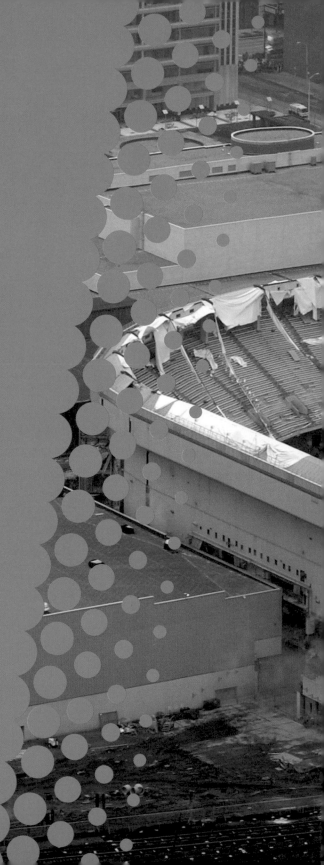

A blast explodes the stadium

into rubble.

BLAM!

Blasting a Bridge

The bridge is weak and rusty.

It has been closed for years.

Many explosions tear apart

the bridge.

BA-DOOM!

The dust clears.

Rubble is all that's left.

Time to clean it up!

Glossary

explode—to blow apart with a loud bang and great force

explosion—a sudden and noisy blowing apart of something

explosive—a chemical that can blow up

rubble—broken bricks, concrete, glass, metal, and other materials left from a building or structure that has fallen down or been destroyed

stadium—a large building in which sports events are held

Read More

Dreier, David. *Be a Demolition Engineer.* Scienceworks! Pleasantville, N.Y.: Gareth Stevens Pub., 2008.

Macken, JoAnn Early. *Demolition.* Construction Zone. Mankato, Minn.: Capstone Press, 2008.

Sutton, Sally. *Demolition.* Somerville, Mass.: Candlewick Press, 2012.

Internet Sites

FactHound offers a safe, fun way to find Internet sites related to this book. All of the sites on FactHound have been researched by our staff.

Here's all you do:

Visit *www.facthound.com*

Type in this code: 9781476520865

Check out projects, games and lots more at
www.capstonekids.com

23

Index

Word Count: 89
Grade: 1
Early-Intervention Level: 13

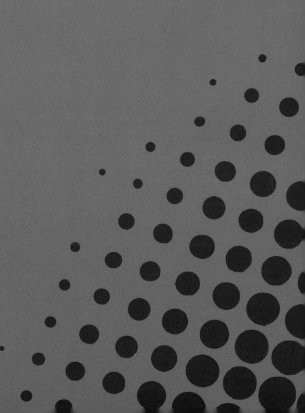